Under the Mulberry Tree:

Poems for & about Raymond Souster

Under the Mulberry Tree:
Poems for & about Raymond Souster

Edited by James Deahl

QUATTRO BOOKS

Copyright © The Contributors and Quattro Books, Inc., 2014

The use of any part of this publication, reproduced, transmitted in any form or by any means, electronic, mechanical, photocopying, or otherwise stored in an electronic retrieval system without the prior consent (as applicable) of the individual author or the designer, is an infringement of the copyright law.

Cover design: Sarah Beaudin
Typography: Grey Wolf Typography
Editor: James Deahl
Consulting Editor: Allan Briesmaster

Library and Archives Canada Cataloguing in Publication

Under the mulberry tree : poems for & about Raymond Souster / James Deahl.

ISBN 978-1-927443-63-7 (pbk.)

    1. Souster, Raymond, 1921-2012--Poetry. 2. Canadian poetry
(English)--21st century. I. Deahl, James, 1945-, editor of compilation,
writer of introduction

PS8279.U5177 2014   C811'.6080351   C2013-907924-6

Published by Quattro Books Inc.
Toronto ON

info@quattrobooks.ca
www.quattrobooks.ca

Printed in Canada

Although it is not the privilege of an editor
to dedicate an anthology of other writers' work,
I believe that the contributors will join me in
dedicating *Under the Mulberry Tree* to Ray's wife.

In book after book over many decades
Ray wrote this simple dedication:

This book is for Rosalia, my Susi, as always.

to which I would like to add these words from Ray's
"Sequence for Susi" which he wrote to celebrate their
40th wedding anniversary.

A simple gold band
fitting snugly on my finger,
which I rub lightly
at least once a day

to remind me that this ring
stands for two,
that only half of it
belongs to me.

Photo by B.M. Litteljohn, courtesy of the League of Canadian Poets

Contents

Simply Ray: an Introduction	11
David Donnell - On Hearing of Ray Souster Pole-Vaulting Over 80	33
Simcha Simchovitch - Raymond Souster	34
Simcha Simchovitch - Downtown	35
Joe Fiorito - Thin Red Line	36
Margaret Patricia Eaton - Battle of Britain — 1940	37
Glen Sorestad - Baseball, One Cold Night in May	38
Brian Purdy - For Ray Souster	41
Lynn Tait - No Envelopes, No Fancy Covers	42
Dennis Lee - sections 82, 86, & 88 from *Riffs*	44
Michael Wurster - Stella By Starlight	46
Michael Wurster - Newsboy	47
Anna Yin - Aftermath	49
David Eso - On Learning Youth Is an Obscene Luxury	50
Michael Fraser - Ray Souster	53
Debbie Okun Hill - The Face of the Banker Poet	54
Laurence Hutchman - Raymond Souster	56
Chris Faiers - The shy man was absent	58
Steven Michael Berzensky - Basho Watching Baseball	60
Bruce Meyer - Obligations	61
Ronnie R. Brown - For Keeps	62
Carleton Wilson - Unlimited Variations on the Avro Lancaster	64
Katherine L. Gordon - Spirit of the City	67
Norma West Linder - Parting Words from a Gentle Man	68
Norma West Linder - Parliament Street	69

Robert Currie - Contact	70
Kent Bowman - Ray Times	71
George Fetherling - Travel	72
Karl Jirgens - Ray drops by for tea	74
S.J. White - Over a Shoulder	76
Bernadette Rule - Grey Matter	77
Andreas Gripp - The Breakfast of Birds	78
Andreas Gripp - Souster's Haiku	79
Laurie Kruk - Luminaries: Aubrey Street, North Bay	80
G.W. Down - A Tip of the Hat to Raymond Souster	82
Ryan Gibbs - Daylight My Darknesses	83
Terry Ann Carter - riding the horse/again	84
Allan Cooper - Ruby-Throated Hummingbird	85
James Deahl - Autumn Ducks, Five O'Clock	86
James Deahl - Japanese Maple	87
John Robert Colombo - The First Poet… and the Foremost	88
Contributors	91
Acknowledgements	99

Raymond Souster in his University of Toronto Schools uniform. UTS is an independent secondary school affiliated with the University of Toronto.
Ray attended high school there.

Photo courtesy of Oberon Press

Simply Ray: an Introduction

WHEN I MOVED TO CANADA during the spring of 1970, an obscure, scarcely published American poet of twenty-four, I knew of virtually no Canadian poets, and those few by reputation only. It has been my great good fortune to have had many Canadian poets befriend me over the past four decades. Several of them became long-term friends, our friendships ending only with their deaths: Milton Acorn, Dorothy Livesay, Ted Plantos, Al Purdy, and Raymond Souster. No poet learns the craft without help and sage advice from those who have already achieved a higher level of writing. As my poetry slowly developed, I learned a great deal from the poets who took me under their wings: Irving Layton, Milton Acorn, and Ray Souster chief among them.

I was honoured to be invited to contribute both prose and poetry to the Al Purdy tribute anthology, *And Left a Place To Stand On*, and it was my privilege to edit Milton Acorn's tribute anthology, *The Northern Red Oak*. Now Ray Souster has died. No anthology can come close to celebrating the life and work of such an important, indeed *essential*, figure in the history of Canadian literature; several large books would be required. But my publisher and I will do our best.

Raymond Holmes Souster, OC, was born in Toronto on January 15, 1921 to Norma and Austin Souster. He died in the city of his birth on October 19, 2012 at the age of ninety-one. Ray spent his entire life in Toronto except for the years during which he saw active duty with the Royal Canadian Air Force during World War II. He served from November 11, 1941 until the end of hostilities, being based first in eastern Canada and later in England. His military experiences would result in his two novels: *The Winter of Time* (published in 1949) and *On Target* (1972). When not serving his country in uniform, he spent his entire working life at the Canadian Imperial Bank of Commerce, from 1939 until his forced retirement. (I say forced because Ray would have kept working had not retirement been mandatory in those days.)

I will briefly cover the principal aspects of the literary life of this seminal poet. These will fall into eight areas: Poetry, Fiction, Editing (both books and magazines), Book Publishing, Organizing Readings, the League of Canadian Poets, Mentorship, and the Souster Legacy. I will start with his own poetry and fiction because Ray was, first and foremost, a writer. Strictly in terms of his own books, and excluding all of his other major accomplishments, Ray can be placed among the most important dozen poets of 20th Century Canada. A final section will deal with his character. I will also refer to him simply as Ray because that is how my friend would wish to be known.

1. Poetry

From his initial magazine appearances to his final poem written on October 5, 2012, Ray was a working poet for seventy-two years. Between 1946 and 2012, he published some fifty-eight books and chapbooks of original poetry (not counting the ten-volume *Collected Poems of Raymond Souster* from Oberon Press, which is essential reading for anyone interested in fine poetry).

Ray launched his professional publishing career in 1946 when John Sutherland's First Statement Press issued his chapbook *When We Are Young*. With First Statement, Ray joined other young poets such as Irving Layton, Miriam Waddington, and Patrick Anderson, all active within the Montreal literary community at the time. It was via this connection to Montreal that Ray formed his extremely important friendships with Louis Dudek and Layton.

Ray was among the first Canadian poets to be inspired by the Populist Poetry of the Chicago School. His major early influences were Kenneth Fearing, Kenneth Patchen, and Carl Sandburg. To a much lesser degree, the influence of Kenneth Rexroth, who was not really part of the Populist movement, can be discerned. Indeed, it was Ray who introduced Milton Acorn, Al Purdy, and several other Canadian People's Poets to American Populism. What appealed to Ray was the mixture of image-based poetry with realism. Such poems would utilize plain speech, and avoid Classical or academic references. This poetry could easily embrace both urban and rural themes, both social-political issues and nature.

Terry Barker has argued in his unpublished paper "Raymond Souster: Compact Canadian Chesterton?" that Ray could be seen as the "father" of People's Poetry in Canada because it was Ray who introduced his fellow poets to Midwest Populist Poetry, especially the work of Fearing and Patchen. Ray was avidly reading books by the American Populists, which he bought mail-order from New York while serving in the RCAF, a few years before he met Irving Layton during the summer of 1943, as well as other young Montreal poets such as Louis Dudek. Indeed, not only can one see many echoes of Fearing in Ray's own poetry, as conclusively demonstrated in Hugh Cook's unpublished M.A. thesis, "The Poetry of Raymond Souster", one can see the same echoes in the early poetry of Irving Layton, Milton Acorn, and Al Purdy, along with other members of Ray's literary circle.

It was in the United States, not Canada, where Ray found his initial success and, more importantly, *encouragement*, publishing poetry in the *Sunday Journal* (Providence, Rhode Island) and the *New York Herald Tribune* (which reprinted a Souster poem from the *Sunday Journal*). Interestingly enough, the editor of the *Sunday Journal* who was so welcoming to the unknown Canadian poet was poet and literary critic Winfield Townley Scott (who would himself later write for the *Herald Tribune* in praise of Carl Sandburg). It was Ray's early interest in the American poets that attracted him to the *First Statement* group rather than to the more British-influenced *Preview* group, the dueling literary movements in Montreal during the first half of the 1940s.

While Fearing, whose poetry Ray discovered in 1939-40 (according to Ray's own account), was the first powerful influence on Ray's mature work, it would be Patchen who would provide the lasting influence. (Ray read Fearing during his RCAF service. Fearing's *Dead Reckoning* had been published in 1938 and his *Collected Poems* two years later. Both were important books for Ray.) Ray developed his poetics throughout the 1940s and 1950s. That is to say, he became better and better at his craft while deepening his vision of Canada. The next big change came in the 1960s after he came across Robert Lowell's *Life Studies* (published in 1959). Throughout the 1960s Ray read Lowell, and by the publication of *Change-Up* (1974) Ray had fully absorbed Lowell's discursive, off-hand, chatty style, which he used for his own purposes. (Always shy and reserved, Ray would write no Confessional poetry.)

Another Chicago-born (but New York-raised) poet who influenced Ray a bit later on during the middle of his career was Harvey Shapiro, whose *This World* (1971) and especially his *National Cold Storage Company* (1988) impressed Ray greatly. Unlike Lowell's *Life Studies*, Shapiro's poetry was tighter and more controlled. This was much like Ray's own pre-*Life Studies* work, and the Shapiro influence was, in my opinion, most beneficial. Indeed, I believe it was Shapiro's poetry that helped reintroduce Ray to the shorter, sharper poetry he had perfected during the 1940s and '50s. Among the many gifts Ray gave to me was a copy of *National Cold Storage Company*.

The final evolution in Ray's poetics demonstrates the continued influence of Patchen. Starting with three collections published during 2006 — *Uptown Downtown, Wondrous Wobbly World,* and *Down to Earth* — Ray began to adopt the brief, imagistic and/or epigramatical poetry that he first discovered in collections like Patchen's *Cloth of the Tempest* (1943). While it is true that he had experimented with this style many years before, in the 21st Century it became a major feature of his poetry. By doing this, Ray was able to focus on wry, witty, and ironic statements, often on aging (his), cultural decay (Toronto's), and corruption (political). In these short pieces, Ray could be at once pithy and humorous, wise and silly. Indeed, he titled many of them "Silly Little Poem No. __." These tiny poems, some of only a single line, could deal with death, religion, beauty, crime, and, quite often, love. Ray never allowed the short form to imprison his vision or in any way to limit his content.

The poetics adopted by Ray were largely, but *not* exclusively, those of the different strands of American Modernism. He was, for example, influenced by a few of the Georgian Poets, Edward Thomas for one, W.W. Gibson for another. And Ray closely read Rainer Maria Rilke. (One must look long and hard to find any Rilke in Ray's later poetry, but it was Rilke's Romanticism that caught Ray's attention. And Ray always had a notable streak of Romanticism in his work.) The Edward Thomas influence is readily found in Ray's nature poetry, both his celebrated "backyard" poems and his Humber River valley poems. The Gibson influence is more in the way of content and poetic stance.

When Oscar Peterson died, both Ray and I were upset when some foolish commentator (supposedly an expert on jazz) claimed that Peterson had been "a great imitator, but *not* a great innovator." It is not my purpose here to dismiss my friend as merely an imitator of American Populist Poetry or any such thing. What Ray took from Kenneth Fearing, Kenneth Patchen, Carl Sandburg, Robert Lowell, Harvey Shapiro, William Carlos Williams, the Georgian Poets, Rilke, etc. he made his own. He used his own creative brilliance to extend their literary ideas. Moreover, Ray was Canadian through and through, his poetry being rooted in our history and literary traditions, especially our Confederation Poets.

Lest my comments be put down as the special pleadings of a personal friend, please consider the following. Just as it is highly unlikely that Oscar Peterson won a Grammy Award for Best Improvised Jazz Solo because he was merely imitating Art Tatum, it is also unlikely Ray won the Governor General's Award for Poetry (in 1964), the Centennial Medal (1967), the City of Toronto Book Award (1979), or was presented with the Order of Canada (1995) because he was imitating Fearing or Patchen. In an era when Canadian poetry was largely unknown in the U.S., Ray's books were read and admired by such poets as Louis Zukofsky, Denise Levertov, Cid Corman, and Larry Eigner. I suspect that back then, Ray and Irving Layton might have been the only Canadian poets widely read by American poets.

While Ray's chosen topics — love, nature, war, social injustice, jazz, religion, and beauty — are universal, he sticks close to Canada and his beloved Toronto. He fully shares a belief in "good common sense" with his Populist Poet cousins. And like them, Ray also believed in the basic goodness of his fellow humans. His life and work were sustained by three pillars: his love for his wife Rosalia, his Christian faith, and his confidence in the power of sharp and decisive poetry. Ray was no Pollyanna, however; as a Christian he fully recognized the action of evil in this world.

Love poetry — Like all real poets, Ray wrote love poems throughout his career. The better pieces, including an entire book of them (*The Eyes of Love*, 1987), date from his marriage to Rosalia, to whom he was devoted. In fact, the romance of Ray and Rosalia is a love story for the ages.

Nature poetry — Striking nature images appear in Ray's poetry from the very beginning. Examples: the rain in "Night of Rain" and the crickets in "The Invaders," both included in *Unit of Five* (1944). The natural world is used in two main ways, as accents to remind the reader of beauty in poems that deal with other, often less pleasant, concerns, and in poems directly about the joy, or heartless cruelty, of fallen nature. Ray's pure nature poems are usually set not far from home: in the Humber River valley or in his own backyard on Baby Point Road. In my reading of Canadian poetry, only Milton Acorn wrote nature poems, and poems highlighting natural images, that were equal to Ray's poetry at its best. When it comes to the backyard poetry from his years on Baby Point, Ray became a Canadian Emily Dickinson.

War poetry — Ray wrote on the horror of war all his life. Most of the poems in *Unit of Five* and much of the poetry in *When We Are Young* (1946) relate to his years in the Air Force during the war. In addition to numerous short poems, Ray wrote a 154-page poem about the ill-conceived raid on Dieppe (August 19, 1942), *Jubilee of Death*, and a 398-page poem, *What Men Will Die For,* about the French war in Vietnam (November 1946-May 1954). The latter was written between February 2001 and March 2007, and is a true epic poem. It was published in 2007.

Jubilee of Death was published in 1984, just a couple of years after I first met Ray. At the time we became friends, Ray was still with the Canadian Imperial Bank of Commerce and I was a financial analyst on Bay Street. To put it another way, we were both paid to look after other people's money. Upon occasion we would meet for lunch. It was at one of these luncheons that Ray gave me a copy of his just-published *Jubilee of Death*. Then, as now, I enjoyed getting into bed with a book to read for half an hour before the arrival of sleep. That night it was *Jubilee of Death*. I admit I was daunted by a 154-page poem, but I thought I would read fifteen pages or so. Ray's poem was so compelling that I read the entire thing, staying up all night, and going to the office the next morning without having slept.

Social poetry — Ray commented on social/political issues from his first publications until the end of his life. Poverty, oppression, violence, racism, anti-Semitism, avarice, and human degeneration were all targets of his poetry. Politically, Ray was well within the spectrum of large "L" liberalism – social democracy. I suspect he always voted N.D.P. once the N.D.P. was created, and he was a passionate supporter of Jack Layton. This was in keeping with his United Church faith. Ray believed that Christians have a social duty. He was a People's Poet from day one, and never wavered in his defense of human dignity.

Jazz poetry — From boyhood Ray was a jazz fan, and he became an expert on the topic. One of his early, and successful, jazz poems is "Salute to Bobby Hackett" (collected in *Cerberus*, 1952). Among his last is "Vic Dickinson" (collected in *Easy Does It*, 2012). He wrote poems referring to jazz in general or about specific jazz players regularly for decades, with what was perhaps his finest hour coming in the eleven-section "No Sad Songs Wanted Here: The Life & Death of the Colonial Bar & Grill," the title sequence of a book Oberon published in 1995.

Religious poetry — While Ray published very little religious poetry, he did write more in his final few years. In his 2011 collection *Big Smoke Blues*, published a year and a half before his death, Ray offered five poems concerning his Christian faith. In "This Man of April" he affirms the presence of Jesus within our lives in this Easter meditation:

> This Man of April
> lives here
> with us still

The poet states in "At Peace" that he has found solace in the arms of Jesus:

> he's found peace
> nestled in
> to his saviour's
> all compassionate grace.

(Throughout *Big Smoke Blues* as a whole, Ray habitually referred to himself in the third person.) Ray was a longtime member of Runnymede United Church.

His final collection of short poems, *Easy Does It* (2012), contains more meditations on mortality and even one on Divine forgiveness. One fine example is "Judgement Day." And there is another Easter meditation, "Good Friday, 2011," in my opinion Ray's finest religious poem.

Beauty — Ray believed (as I do) that the existence of beauty, and the ability of humans to see and appreciate it, is a proof of the basic goodness of creation in general, and of mankind in particular. Beauty has redemptive qualities that are needed in this defiled world. Ray often opposed the city with all its faults and blemishes to the pure beauty of trees, flowers, rivers, sunsets, and birds. Until he became old and unstable on his feet, Ray would often walk by the Humber River, which flows quite near his home on Baby Point. He especially enjoyed Étienne Brûlé Park, the Old Mill area, and Lambton Woods.

An excellent example of how Ray contrasted natural beauty with the corrupt, dispiriting city is "Nocturnal" from 1940. Another, written sixty years later, is "Black Trillium" (from *Of Time & Toronto*, 2000). In the latter piece, a single flower can "spread a welcome veil of peace / across the battered face / of a despairing world."

In terms of literary quality alone, I place Ray among the finest dozen or so Canadian poets of the 20th Century, and certainly well into the Top Ten Canadian poets of the post-World War II period. And I write here only about his poetry. Between *When We Are Young* (First Statement Press, 1946) and *Never Counting the Cost* (The Battered Silicon Dispatch Box, 2012), Ray published fifty-six other books and chapbooks of poetry.

While it is not my intention to write a critical essay on Ray's poetry, allow me to close this section with my personal observation. Some critics are of the opinion that Ray began to write his really good poetry only during the very late 1950s-early 1960s, perhaps around the time he wrote the poems included in *A Local Pride* (published in 1962). This opinion, in my view, is in error. Ray's section of *Unit of Five* offers the reader several poems of remarkable quality, "Night of Rain," "Ten PM," "Hunger," "Search," and "Reality" being five examples. Because *Unit of Five* was published in 1944, all of Ray's poems were written during his stint with the RCAF. And *When We Are Young* (1946) has numerous fine pieces. "The Hunter," "The Lagoon," "Waiting," and "The Barracks" are, in my opinion, as worthy of praise as any poetry being written at the time by anyone else in Canada. And this just takes us to the close of World War II. By the time *For What Time Slays* appeared in 1955, Ray had published so many excellent poems that they are too numerous to list here.

But you need not take my word for this. Prof. Francis Mansbridge locates the start of the good, mature poetry as early as "The Penny Flute," first published in 1941 (and collected in *When We Are Young*, 1946). Hugh Cook considers "Night Watch," "Air Raid," and "Apple Blow" to be among the first of Ray's poems to display lasting quality (published in 1943). Ray's choice would be the aforementioned "Nocturnal," first published in 1940.

I fully agree with Ray. "Nocturnal" surely must count among the outstanding poems to be published that year in Canada. Although published in the *Canadian Forum* in 1940, it was not to appear in book form until Ray's *Go to Sleep, World* (1947). To understand just how strong Ray's poetry was when he was still quite a young man, I highly recommend the *Collected Poems of Raymond Souster, Volume One, 1940-55*. Not many poets write major poems prior to the age of twenty. But Ray did.

I have read the forty-seven books and chapbooks of Ray's poetry I own. I have also read his two novels. It is my personal taste in poetry — and only my personal taste — that prompts these next statements. I prefer the poems Ray wrote before the influence of Robert Lowell's *Life Studies*; these early poems are often great, as fine as any poems written in Canada. I also like reading the longer, more discursive poems Ray wrote after he had read and digested *Life Studies*, but not as much. I feel that Ray was at his best when he wrote shorter, more imagistic poems. (I feel I must note here that many critics believe exactly the opposite.) Finally, I am much less interested in Ray's post-Oberon poems (2004-2012), but would like to make it clear that there are a great many good poems in Ray's final books, all published by The Battered Silicon Dispatch Box. Among these final sixteen titles the reader will find *What Men Will Die For*, which is compelling reading. The longer, looser line served Ray well when he wrote of war.

As I have stated above, Ray wrote first-rate poetry from 1940 until his death in 2012. Not one of his sixty books is a bad book, some are just better than others. All are worth reading. I eagerly await the publication of a truly definitive *Selected Poems of Raymond Souster, 1940-2012*. It will be an exceedingly fine book by any standards.

2. Fiction

Ray wrote two novels: *The Winter of Time* (published under the *nom de plume* Raymond Holmes in 1949, re-published in 2006) and *On Target* (published under the *nom de plume* John Holmes in 1972, re-published in 2006). The first is a short novel, the latter ninety pages longer. Both deserve to be read.

The Winter of Time is a coming of age tale set against the backdrop of World War II. *On Target*, also set during the war, is largely based on the flight log and wartime experiences of one of Ray's comrades-at-arms in the Air Force. In the opinion of the present writer, *The Winter of Time* is quite a good, well-written book; *On Target* is a major achievement. Clearly Ray was a gifted novelist as well as a gifted poet, although Ray's fiction does fall short of the true excellence his finest poetry achieved.

Both of these novels use the realistic, straight-forward storytelling perfected by Morley Callaghan and James T. Farrell. If you like a well-told story of the human drama of young men caught up in a war they did not start and may not live to finish, a tale of blind courage and heartbreak, of clinging to life with raw determination, buy and read *On Target*.

3. Editing (both books and magazines)

Through his textbooks as well as volumes like *100 Poems of Nineteenth-Century Canada, Comfort of the Fields, Vapour and Blue, Powassan's Drum*, and *Windflower*, Ray established himself as a leading expert on Canadian poetry from the Confederation period to the emerging poets of 1980.

Five volumes of 19th Century poetry (three co-edited by Douglas Lochhead): *100 Poems of Nineteenth Century Canada*, with Lochhead (Macmillan of Canada, 1974), *Vapour and Blue: the poetry of William Wilfred Campbell* (Paget Press, 1978), *Comfort of the Fields: Archibald Lampman, best-known Poems* (Paget Press, 1979), *Powassan's Drum: Selected Poems of Duncan Campbell Scott*, with Lochhead (Tecumseh, 1985), and *Windflower: Poems of Bliss Carman*, with Lochhead (Tecumseh, 1985).

Unfortunately, I have only two of these, the selections from Archibald Lampman (*Comfort of the Fields*) and the selections from W.W. Campbell (*Vapour and Blue*). Both are quite fine representations of these two major poets. I certainly wish I had the three that were co-edited by Douglas Lochhead, but I have never found them in any used bookshop. I do not understand how I missed out on the final two volumes because Ray and I were good friends by 1985.

Four textbooks (all co-edited by Richard Woolatt): *Generation Now* (Longman Canada, 1970), *Sights and Sounds* (Macmillan of Canada, 1973), *These loved, these hated lands* (Doubleday Canada, 1975), and *Poems of A Snow-Eyed Country* (Academic Press, 1980).

Between 1970 and the early 1980s it is quite likely that a student in Ontario would meet one of the textbooks edited by Ray and Richard Woolatt. The first one, *Generation Now*, like the other three, is entirely poetry. It includes work from Canadian, American, and British writers. It is no surprise that Souster favourites Kenneth Patchen, William Carlos Williams, Carl Sandburg, W.W. Gibson, Edward Thomas, Kenneth Fearing, and Kenneth Rexroth are well represented.

Sights and Sounds is also international, but with a much tighter focus on American and Canadian poets, including Milton Acorn, Carl Sandburg, Gwendolyn MacEwen, and Robert Frost. This textbook also includes one of the rare poems by Ray's mentor Winfield Townley Scott.

Spanish-language and French-Canadian poets play a prominent role in *These loved, these hated lands*. Examples are Salvador Diaz Miron, Octavio Paz, Jose Juan Tablada, Jacques Brault, Roland Giguère, Anne Hébert, Gilles Hénault, Gatien Lapointe, Hector de Saint-Denys-Garneau, and Pierre Trottier.

The final textbook Richard Woolatt and Ray edited is entirely Canadian, with a strong French-Canadian presence. *Poems of A Snow-Eyed Country* introduces several poets of the (then) younger generation: Tom Howe, Hans Jewinski, Sid Marty, Joseph Sherman, Andrew Suknaski, Peter Van Toorn, Tom Wayman, and Dale Zieroth.

I own copies of all four books. As a former teacher of Canadian literature at the high school and college levels, I can attest to their excellence. Had I been teaching during the 1970-1985 period I would have wanted to use them with my students. I can also report that my three daughters were not given such finely-edited books when they attended high school in Ontario during the post-1985 years. Although these were edited and published for school children, they would be enjoyed and valued by adult readers. These books certainly refuse to talk down to their intended audience simply because they are teenagers. If only today's textbooks would treat students like intelligent people. I know I liked reading them and can recommend them to readers of all ages.

Four literary magazines: *Direction*, 1943-1946, *Enterprise*, 1948, *Contact*, 1952-1954, and *Combustion*, 1957-1960. Of these magazines, the latter two were truly important, and not simply for Canadian poets. Both *Contact* and *Combustion* attracted readers and contributors from outside Canada. Among the regular readers of *Contact* were Americans Larry Eigner, Louis Zukofsky, Theodore Holmes, Robert Creeley, and Donald M. Allen. Readers of *Combustion* included Denise Levertov and Eigner. As noted by Cook in his M.A. thesis, *Contact* would publish the work of Canadians Dudek, Layton, and Alfred G. Bailey, Americans Charles Olson, Robert Creeley, Paul Blackburn, Lawrence Ferlinghetti, and Cid Corman, as well as leading non-English-language poets in translation: Octavio Paz,

Jacques Prévert, Guillaume Apollinaire, Gottfried Benn, Jean Cocteau, Anna Akhmatova, and George Seferis.

Combustion, like *Contact*, was also international in scope. Contributors included Gary Snyder, Robert Duncan, Fielding Dawson, Zukofsky, and Creeley. Denise Levertov's *With Eyes in the Back of Our Heads*, for one example, includes poems initially published in both *Contact* and *Combustion*. And poems in Gary Snyder's *The Back Country* first appeared in *Combustion*. Indeed, Frank Davey has written that "*Combustion* made a significant contribution to U.S. literature." Prof. Davey also wrote that "*Contact* was thus the first Canadian magazine to publish U.S. poets of the Black Mountain school."

What Ray was able to do was place Canadian poetry before the world and introduce foreign poets to Canadians. In my view, *Contact* and *Combustion* were the most important Canadian poetry magazines of the 1960s, an opinion shared by Donald M. Allen and several U.S. poets.

Three anthologies of contemporary poetry: *Poets 56: Ten Younger English-Canadians* (Contact Press, 1956), *New Wave Canada: The New Explosion in Canadian Poetry* (Contact Press, 1966), and *Made in Canada: New Poems of the Seventies*, with Douglas Lochhead (Oberon Press, 1970).

I own only one of these anthologies, *Made in Canada: New Poems of the Seventies*, which I bought as soon as it was published. This was my first, serious introduction to Canadian poetry, and it was through this volume that I, as a brand new immigrant in 1970, got to know the poetry of Milton Acorn, Margaret Atwood, Earle Birney, bill bissett, David Donnell, Paul Dutton, Doug (now George) Fetherling, Patrick Lane, Dennis Lee, Dorothy Livesay, Gwendolyn MacEwen, Ray himself, Francis Sparshott, Colleen Thibaudeau, and Robert Zend prior to becoming acquainted with, and in many cases close friends with, the poets themselves. This was an eye-opening anthology, and one of the best-edited in Canada, then or now.

As he would do a decade later with his textbook *Poems of A Snow-Eyed Country*, Ray included no fewer than twenty young, emerging poets in with Governor General's Award-winning poets Margaret Atwood, Earle Birney, Dorothy Livesay, Eli Mandel, Alden Nowlan, P.K. Page, and Ray himself. Three of these young poets — David Donnell, George Fetherling, and Dennis Lee — have contributed to the present anthology.

No editor could discover talented poets like Ray. At least fifteen of the poets introduced to the public in *Made in Canada* had yet to publish their first collections, and a good many others had only a single publication to their credit. Of the previously "unknown" poets, some half a dozen have seen their poetry installed in the CanLit canon, eight would have their poetry appear in *The New Oxford Book of Canadian Verse in English* (1983 edition), and one has gone on to win the Governor General's Award for Poetry. A good many of today's leading poets owe a great deal to Ray's editing and/or publishing genius.

If the two Contact Press anthologies are as valuable as *Made in Canada*, I wish I had them.

4. Book Publishing

Contact Press, established by Ray, Louis Dudek, and Irving Layton, ran for fifteen years (1952-1967). Authors published include Milton Acorn, Margaret Atwood, George Bowering, Leonard Cohen, Frank Davey, Louis Dudek, George Ellenbogen, Eldon Grier, Daryl Hine, D.G. Jones, Irving Layton, Gwendolyn MacEwen, Eli Mandel, Kenneth McRobbie, John Newlove, Alden Nowlan, Al Purdy, Gael Turnbull, and Phyllis Webb. Sometimes their Contact Press book was the first professional publication these poets had. Almost all are now firmly ensconced in the canon of major Canadian poets, yet most were unknown when Contact Press published them.

5. Organizing Public Readings

As a direct outgrowth of *Contact* magazine, for many years Ray organized and hosted dozens of poetry readings in Toronto, initially at the Isaacs Gallery, and finally, decades later, at the University of Toronto in the mid-1980s. As with *Contact*, Ray featured Canadian poets from all regions across our vast country, Leonard Cohen, Al Purdy, Alden Nowlan, and James Reaney among them, as well as such major American poets as Charles Olson, Denise Levertov, Robert Creeley, LeRoi Jones (as he was known then), Louis Zukofsky, Frank O'Hara, and Cid Corman. In many cases, this would be the first Canadian reading for the Americans and the first Toronto reading for the Canadians. These readings Ray organized were the most important in the Toronto-area until Greg Gatenby built the Harbourfront Reading Series into one of the finest and most comprehensive in the world.

Ray even worked poems by Levertov, Creeley, and O'Hara into his textbooks for Ontario schools. Through poetry readings, magazines, and textbook anthologies, Ray introduced the general public and students to a wide and eclectic variety of Canadian, American, British, and non-English-language writers. As I recall, one of the readings Ray hosted at the University of Toronto (University College) was my first appearance at that university.

6. The League of Canadian Poets

The founding of The League of Canadian Poets dates from August 20, 1966 when Ray along with Louis Dudek, Ronald G. Everson, and Michael Gnarowski met with Ralph Gustafson at the latter's home in North Hatley, Quebec. The LCP grew out of that meeting, and Ray served as its first President (then called Chairman), 1967-1971. It's doubtful if the LCP would exist without Ray's dedicated work during its early, formative years. (The reader may wish to consult *Making the Damn Thing Work* by Raymond

Souster, published for the 35th birthday of the League of Canadian Poets.)

7. Mentorship

Ray had unlimited time and energy when it came to encouraging other writers. During the thirty years I knew Ray he spent as much energy, if not more, helping and promoting other poets than he spent on his own writing. Contributors Sam Simchovitch and Carleton Wilson are but two examples of poets Ray assisted, either by mail (Sam) or in person (Carleton). Others included Gwendolyn MacEwen and Alden Nowlan. Poets who have praised Ray's support are countless; Michael Ondaatje has written, "He brought many of us to the surface and we owe him everything."

8. The Souster Legacy

Two of the poets who have generously contributed to this tribute anthology — Simcha (Sam) Simchovitch and Norma West Linder — are among the leading Sousterian poets writing today. Sam was born in Poland the same day as Ray, January 15, 1921, and Ray always referred to Sam is his "poet-twin." Norma was born later that same decade, and was inspired to write poetry by reading Ray's work. Both of these poets have, of course, made their own significant contributions to Canadian letters, both in poetry and prose. And both carry on the literary tradition Ray started some 65 years ago. The Souster legacy extends far beyond these two writers, however. One can clearly see Ray's influence on the poetry of Milton Acorn, for example. And I have also learned a great deal from Ray and his poetry, as have contributors such as Kent Bowman and Michael Fraser.

In addition, such public appreciation as exists for the work of Confederation Poets Archibald Lampman (Ray's favourite Canadian poet), William Wilfred Campbell,

Duncan Campbell Scott, and Bliss Carman can be largely traced to the volumes of their work Ray so painstakingly edited, some on his own and some with Douglas Lochhead.

9. The Man Himself

Ray was a true gentleman of the old school as well as a man of honour in the full sense of the word. The terms "gentleman" and "honour" might sound odd these days, but they have real meaning. When I think of Ray, as I often do, certain words like courage, compassion, honesty, generosity, and strength leap into my mind. The poetry world is, sad to say, populated by sharp operators. Ray was never among them. Ray believed in cooperation, not competition, among writers. As a poet, editor, and publisher he was strikingly honest. A hallmark feature of his writing was his social commitment to, and deep compassion for, his fellow humans.

Ray faced many hardships throughout his long life that I need not go into here. A tribute anthology is no place to rehearse this modest man's personal trials. I will mention only the three that many of his readers already know about. Ray went blind, and despite becoming blind, which he expected to happen, he kept on with his usual daily life as long as possible. He wrote hundreds of poems after he lost his sight. Every time I visited him, Ray was in a good mood. He accepted his condition, and did not allow it to depress or define him.

Prior to going blind, Ray lost all his teeth. For several years he was reduced to eating puréed baby food. Around this time he had to stop drinking beer and wine. All readers of Ray's poetry or fiction will know how attached he was to the pleasures of the table. With the loss of his sight and the loss of his teeth, his world became very narrow. Again, I never heard him complain.

I assure my readers that his blindness and the loss of his teeth were not the greatest of his burdens.

The third thing was death. It was Ray's fate to suffer what the Irish call a hard death. During his last three years he was often in pain, and sometimes his pain was quite severe. On the rare occasions when he mentioned his physical sufferings he did so as if merely recounting a fact. I never heard him complain. The details of his ninety-one years in this world were the actions of Providence. The pains and the pleasures were to be equally accepted.

One of the results of living for nine decades is that most of your friends die before you. Almost all of Ray's friends and colleagues who were born during the 1920s and 1930s are gone. Were they still with us, I am certain this anthology would contain work by Milton Acorn, Earle Birney, Fred Cogswell, Cid Corman, Louis Dudek, Ronald G. Everson, Ralph Gustafson, Irving Layton, Denise Levertov, Douglas Lochhead, Charles Olson, Al Purdy, James Reaney, and John Sutherland, to mention a few of Ray's buddies.

Even ignoring all of his literary achievements, Ray was a great man. He was a rare and true example of how to fully *live* a life. I consider it to have been a privilege and a blessing to have been his friend.

Given Ray's humility, he would no doubt think I have gone on far too long. He would much rather praise other poets than have us praise him. So I had better turn this over to the other contributors.

James Deahl
Sarnia, 2013

A Note on the Title

Readers of Ray's poetry will know that a giant mulberry tree dominated his large backyard on Baby Point. It is mentioned in many of his poems. Following Ray's retirement from the bank, he would host "poetry afternoons" during the summer under this tree. It is at these gatherings we would sip beer and discuss the poetry of Patchen, Fearing, Lowell, Purdy, Acorn, Dudek, and Lampman. And as I write this I clearly see Ray, beer in hand, holding forth on the Confederation Poets. I hope there are mulberry trees in Heaven.

    J.D.

Raymond Souster at age 50

Photo courtesy of Oberon Press

On Hearing of Ray Souster Pole-Vaulting Over 80

David Donnell

Denise Levertov's first book was called *Here &*
Now. Here &
            then, now & when. I still remember playing

ping pong with you one night at a writer's party in 1961
at some upscale house with a big rec room in the basement.

Some time around the anthology *New Wave Canada*. Some time
before you published your 10th or 15th book *Ten*
                                  Elephants
on Yonge Street. Now is where, & now it's January
& I can smell spring in the air all over the great Metropolis.

Burning orange crates in your back yard after supper some
evening this May or June
                     take a look south at where
the Humber empties into Lake Ontario & think of how unlucky
O'Hara was. You were a nice guy, you let me win.

Thanks a lot for your wise advice, & many happy returns.

Raymond Souster

Simcha Simchovitch

The lustre of common words,
the splendour of ordinary people
radiates from your poems.
Your verse breathes compassion
for every creature on earth.

Poet of everyday life,
daytime at banker's desk,
evening in darkened tavern,
tuning in to the music
of workingmen's talk.

Downtown, in rush hour,
when stone-and-glass structures
disgorge the city's multitudes,
you alone distinguish
among the throngs
the drunk Indian lad, muttering
his unheard complaint
or the tall Slav inveighing
against this wasteland of a city.

Raymond Souster, master
of keen and simple verse
that hallow every hour
of our mundane existence.

Downtown

SIMCHA SIMCHOVITCH

Downtown streets of the metropolis
amid business rush replete
with unemployed, drifters, welfare bums;
in polluted parks and squares,
on benches, sprawled on the grass,
in the sun they warm their bodies.

Comes evening, daytime clatter
subsides amid cooler breezes,
the streets begin to sound and glitter
with neon-lights, the beat of jazz.

From basements, rooming-houses, attics
creatures crawl to partake
the unholy spectacle:
Pimps and hard-drug pushers,
desperate addicts, old lechers,
runaways from the suburbia;
and, woe to mothers,
daughters in their teens,
awaiting sale-and-kicks
in nooks and doorways.

Thin Red Line

Joe Fiorito

Her finger curls a bit;
she cut the tendon when

she slit her wrist: inevitably,
she'd clenched her fist.

"Next time, I'm doing it like
this." Her palm open,

intent on harm, she mimed
a razor up her arm.

Battle of Britain — 1940

Margaret Patricia Eaton

Another routine night in the hospital,
painting their foreheads with a blue M or a red T,
making sure they don't get a double dose
of morphine or tetanus
and so finish the Luftwaffe's mission.

Air raid sirens sound all clear,
but it's too late for these ones
or the orphan boy — father dead in France,
mother dead in factory ruins,
his sight destroyed by flying glass shards.

Homeless, he wanders the hospital corridors,
seeking his favourite nurse so he can sing to her —
"You are my sunshine."

Baseball, One Cold Night in May
Glen Sorestad

remembering Ray Souster

I've been cold. I live in Saskatchewan where
cold is never very far away, even in July.
Cold is a genuine danger people can
never completely shrug off or ignore.
Cold holds you like childhood memory.
I have had frostbitten ears, nose, hands and feet.
I know the pain of recovery from frost bite.

But I do not believe I have been colder
than one May night in Toronto Ray Souster
and I went out to the old lakefront stadium,
to watch Dave Stieb pitch against the Red Sox.
It must have been the early 1980s and Stieb
was beginning to show how good a pitcher
he was going to be, though he wasn't there yet.

I was in Toronto for literary meetings
and on a whim phoned up Ray to see whether
he might be keen on attending the game,
knowing Souster, apart from being a poet
I greatly admired, was also a student of baseball.
Souster was quick to accept.

The day had been pleasant enough
to walk around wearing a sports coat
and since that was the warmest I had,
I met Souster, so dressed. He looked
a bit dubiously at me, but was too polite
to comment on my strange ball park garb.

After only a few innings the wind began
to rage in off Lake Ontario, muscling its way
into the stands, its wintry breath quick-chilling
summery hotdogs and burgers, icing
our popcorn breath. I realized the folly
of my evening wear. I could hear the voice
of my friend Peter Christensen:
The weather is never wrong, just your clothes.
Souster probably took me for a tough
prairie farm boy, impervious to cold,
though I huddled in my seat, chatting baseball,
trying to avoid chattering teeth
and to disguise my shivering.

It turned out to be a lousy game.
Stieb served up one of his worst efforts,
falling behind in the count to each hitter,
with predictable results. The Beantown Sox
kept themselves warm circling the bases
while the Jays and their fans sat mute
as ice cubes in a freezer tray.

After bidding Souster good night
outside the subway station, I'd have
stolen both second and third bases
with my hustle back to my hotel,
before sliding safely into a warm bed.

August 20, 1966. Initial meeting at the home of Ralph & Betty Gustafson of the founders of The League of Canadian Poets: Louis Dudek, Ronald G. Everson, Mike Gnarowski, Ralph Gustafson, and Raymond Souster.

Pictured here (left to right) are Lorna Everson, Ronald G. Everson, Ralph Gustafson, Rosalia Souster, Raymond Souster, and Louis Dudek.

Photo taken by Betty Gustafson, courtesy of Carleton Wilson

For Ray Souster

BRIAN PURDY

grounds-crew seventy years
for your art, you worked the bank
kept scrupulous double books
— rendered unto Caesar but
honored the snowman witnessed
in a brick-and-tin-can empty lot
slowly filling up with snow
who saw the foot-prints of passers-by
and knew your city. so the poet became
at once, *anonymous*
and omnipresent — elephantine
on yonge street, truest
colour of your time

No Envelopes, No Fancy Covers

Lynn Tait

dedicated to Raymond Souster

Can't believe how much
you and W.C. Williams look alike.
      It's crazy. You could be brothers.
I picture both of you, all rain-slicked in white and red,
like bleeding plasterers who, I assume,
are now mixing words
in some huge wheel barrel in the sky.

All you ever wanted
was to be left alone in the wind,
to be part of all that greenness;
a six-quart basket left in the sunshine,
waiting for snow fruit.

Maybe, you are back
amongst your sacred willows,
a ghost, scaring hidden lovers
with sudden cold breezes
on hot summer evenings,
leaving them with *"one last*
fragile shivering," whipping up
their soft yellow garlands,
their ancient trunks creaking, rusting hinges,
God's hand at the door,
or, are you dropping acorns,
on passers-by from oak-framed streets,
somewhere in Toronto?

I think I'll take your advice
and get this poem outdoors
among the gardens, lilacs, willows,
and my own mulberry tree, still barren,
always the last to leaf,
first to gather birds,
and I will fill my heart with song
though I also have no reason,
same as you —
all my best Christmases are behind me,
but you have taken death without bitterness,
become that lovely new notebook
waiting to be filled.

sections 82, 86, & 88 from *Riffs*

Dennis Lee

82

Rockface
      hallelujah.

Thought-
      high
emergence of

          foothold:

faithful

          : phrase.

86

There is an
        indoors of the selfsame, which
   calls to a straitened heart.

(And hunger.

      Hunger.)

88

The dolphins of need be-
lie their shining traces.
Arcs in the air.

They do not mean to last. One
upward furrow, bright & the long disappearance,

as though by silver fiat of the sea.

Stella By Starlight

MICHAEL WURSTER

Night and an open window fluttering curtain breeze
awakened from my book by Mr. Coltrane's
all the ecstasy power anguish in the world

entrance.

Newsboy

MICHAEL WURSTER

Newsboy
in his fifties
with wild hair
and gray clothing

shivering on the corner
of Fifth and Wood,
hands in pockets,
whistling

"Saint Louis Blues"
out of tune.

Raymond Souster reading from *Jubilee of Death*
at Letters bookshop, 1984.
This was Ray's final public reading.

Photo by Henry Martinuk

Aftermath

Anna Yin

> *reading Ray's "Artificial Hand," "War Veteran"
> and "Broken Bottle"*

After banqueting, the chants fade. Drunken hands
        throw empty bottles.
Under the shining moon, shattered glasses
    in light or shadow   form a picture
like Van Gogh's "Iris," fragile in the wind.

      The only intact bottle
lies by itself, dark eye watching
    the remote smoke.   On the wall
the severed ear listens
      to the moaning from the frontline.
              Iris' petals fall into pieces.

On Learning Youth Is an Obscene Luxury
David Eso

I follow Souster's directions
clean and clear as lines of verse
to Baby Point Road.
Driveway tongue rolls out.
I put the panting engine to rest
look to the unblinking windows
and door, silent mouth of the house.

Knock, knock.

Time bears down hard on the poet:
translucent blue relief
map his face has become
eyes, milky with blinded kindness
back, bent into a query.
Writing hand trails past surfaces
leading to the snow-bright kitchen.
He's lived here for centuries.

Crackle, crackle.

Jazz solos and baseball scores
know their way around the place
from a vintage radio
with wilting antenna.
Earlier drafts
show through the wallpaper.
Smell of tobacco and coffee stains
blueberry yoghurt and medication.
Snow falls against the window
as if there were no other seasons.

A-hem, a-hrumph

dismisses our silence.
Prior to speech, the mind
announcing itself, sharp and severe
listens to me say nothing.
From sequestered darkness
dispenses a scrap of wisdom from the pile:

Old age is not for the wimpy.

November 1982 in Bayview Village Park, Toronto

Photo by Bruce Meyer

Ray Souster

MICHAEL FRASER

Riding my bike to
his Baby Point house,
I watched June tumble
kelly green from burr oaks.

It was 4:30, and I remember traffic
rose full-crest off Jane Street.

Dori introduced me,
then his ears craned to grab my hello.
He stood with gathered years
stacked on his back,
our handshake bridging
air that didn't know it was air,
and the generations caught between us.

I wouldn't say reclusive,
not after he fed me a book
of *Old Bank Notes* which he
rendered sharp from the memory
his blindness enhanced.

To this day, his voice ordains
the words with each cycled page.

The Face of the Banker Poet

Debbie Okun Hill

He stands outdoors
on a sunny day
wearing his banker's best
buttoned up tailored suit
white shirt with a tie
knotted under a chin.

His oval face
almond eyes
hidden by dark
horn-rimmed glasses.

This is what strangers
see on the internet
when they search
for his image.

Raymond Souster.

A reserved man preserved
in a black and white photo.
A dedicated employee of
the Canadian Imperial
Bank of Commerce.
A poet who spent years
surrounded by numbers
moonlighting with his words.

So shy, he remains hidden from fame.
Such a shame!
Won't see his poetic face
plastered on a Canadian bill!

Photo courtesy of the League of Canadian Poets

UNDER THE MULBERRY TREE

Raymond Souster

LAURENCE HUTCHMAN

You were one of the poets who read in a suit
looking like your photo, the banker.
I was drawn to your language
the spare line, the immediate voice
evoking the life of Toronto,
the sleepy summer Humber River,
its hidden secrets couched in lush ravines.

It was my childhood too — being cowboys and Indians
sneaking along the stream under sand cliffs,
the farmers chasing us from apple orchards,
the surreal ride on the Sunnyside roller coaster,
penny arcades, peep shows, Siamese twins in a bottle,
the fish pond where I won a gas mask.

You made me recognize the history around me:
the haunting outline of the Old Mill,
sunken vessels off Hanlan's point
William Lyon Mackenzie rebelling
in his Bond Street house,
your father fighting (as my grandfather had)
in the yellow gases of the Somme.

You captured the moments in still life:
a newsstand man hawking his papers in summer heat,
an aboriginal woman fighting off drunken men,
(I saw them in the bars on Gerrard Street)
the boys shining shoes under palace cinema lights,
the armless war veterans with their medals.
Your words focussed as a light
on the suffering of their faces.
We could not walk past them.

Your poems drawn subtlety
of the desire of lovers
uncovering their shy naked bodies.

No one has painted this city as you have,
made its history our own.

The shy man was absent

CHRIS FAIERS

Raymond Souster Tribute, Nov. 22, 2011

The shy man was absent
from his own poetry tribute
sixty plus of us crammed
the second floor of Runnymede Library
the shy man's bookish retreat
for most of his 90 years

The shy man's imprint was Contact
(irony universal in poetry's ascent)

he made contact with poetry readings
poetry magazines and poetry organizations
poetry of the best, by the best
but poetry for everyone

The shy man slipped his teller's cage
miraculously to birth, with a few close friends
the modern age of Canadian poetry

A bank teller, for God's sake
who never swore, womanized
stole a dime, overwrote a line
Will he even show up for his own funeral?
will we file past an empty casket
the shy man busy elsewhere, composing perhaps

When the shy man passes
to join his legion of friends
in the Canuck poetry pantheon
we earthbound ones will need
a statue or two
to fix his shy spirit a place

beside bronze Al in Queen's Park?
(Al shy? — all poets are shy)
or comfortable yards apart
from an even shyer genius
Glenn on his permanent bench
outside CBC quarters?

until the time of bust in bronze
poet after poet visits Ray
in a nursing home just around
Runnymede's comfortable corner
But tonight the shy man's legacy connects
a tribal gathering of poets his tribute
>> **not one empty chair**

Under the Mulberry Tree

Basho Watching Baseball

Steven Michael Berzensky

*Baseball Haiku & Senryu
for Ray Souster (1921 - 2012)*

Basho watching baseball.
   Now, between innings:
     pen new poems.

During a dull night game
at last the dome opens —
   ah, the full moon!

Root for the home team
   pray for home runs —
homeless man outside
   hand extended.

A fan contemplates
   the meaning of life . . .
in the lull between pitches.

Obligations

BRUCE MEYER

Raymond Souster

A poet's reputation is almost a butterfly —
from pupa to chrysalis, cocoon to wings.

The journey is long and the wind against him.
He must find a home among the fallen trees

and feed on flowers that bloom without him.
Ray was wrapped in white sheets, his eyes

so keen like Milton he had lost his vision,
or Tiresias, a Sibyl in a basket knowing more

than my head could contain. He memorized
my poems, recited works by others as well,

pointed to book stacks he had learned by heart
that went to the bottomless sea of his memory.

Take something with you, he requested. Release
them to the world. The art of being a poet is flight —

not yours, not your ego or even your soul —
but words — words that rise startled at the sound

of daylight on an autumn morning when you
know there is only one direction home and passion

seen in the face of life shrivelling within sends
them home, each wing a beating heart, defying gravity.

For Keeps

Ronnie R. Brown

*Thoughts on the 50th anniversary of
the D-Day invasion, June 6th, 1994.*

The television cameras love them,
track the mottled, vein-corded hand
as it traces the letters
of a fallen comrade's name, zoom
in on a tear as it slides
down a craggy face.

Fifty years ago, the voice-over reminds,
many of these "old soldiers"
were still in their teens.

Moved by patriotism, wanderlust,
or the dream of new boots, three squares
every day and money, too,
they lied about their age, signed
on the line. Children,
some no more than thirteen,
donning uniforms, marching away.

Upstairs, days from turning seventeen,
my own son sits, eyes focused
on the computer's screen. If I listen
I can hear the muted sounds
of explosions, guns, as, joy stick in hand,
he struggles to save some fantasy world
from simulated catastrophe.

I try to convince myself he is safe,
will never wear a uniform, march off,
gun in hand, to defend democracy,
will not come home years later,
changed, as his grandfather did,
will never know the nightmares
that rend a soldier's sleep; try to forget,
if only for a moment, that a click
away, television cameras are focused
on other mothers' children. Live
via satellite they stand, winning smiles
on their adolescent faces,
holding guns
that should be toys,
acting all grown up,
playing for keeps.

Unlimited Variations on the Avro Lancaster
CARLETON WILSON

for Raymond Souster

That evening in your kitchen you talked of the Hogtown
jazz joints you'd once frequented. The portable radio

propped in the counter's corner sputtered out all the old
war standards, and now and then you'd pipe up about

this certain piece being performed, the instrument
featured and the player for whom you held such

admiration. For my part, I couldn't add much, just
ask questions and note down the names of musicians

I should listen to, their Vanguard Records I might
find now on CD. This is how I recall that spring night,

with Duke Ellington crowding the elbow room of your
kitchen table all the way back from the 1960s

stage at Massey Hall, and Bobby Hackett hunched over
in the doorway blowing his horn — a song you'd requested

he play once long ago in the Town Tavern at Queen
and Yonge. Earlier, as I read through your *Selected Poems*,

I'd glimpsed that past world, caught hold of
Old Toronto between the lines, as it had been

back when streetcars seemed red rockets hurtling across
a gridded universe. And there in the radio's tinny wake,

the electric kettle counterpoint, a low timpani murmur
in the background, I watched as you picked up a postcard

of a Lancaster bomber from amongst your papers,
a picture that reminded you of an American poet,

a bombardier during the war, who'd returned to the village
in Italy where he'd flown, wept on a stranger's steps

with his wife, as you did then while telling his account.
The water's boil soon added its breathy, high-pitched

whistle to the evening's arrangements and you went
to tend to the tea, while I was left steeped in thoughts

of my best friend's grandfather who flew in the war —
a tail-gunner in a Lanc who'd kicked out the scratched

Perspex panels of his turret just to see the Messerschmitts
better; and my own grandfather who'd commanded a tank

from Normandy to Apeldoorn, and survived the ordeal,
though he left his final battle wounded, a time bomb inside

him that went off seventeen years later. These things seeped
into the mind as you placed teapot and cups on the table,

sat again with me in the kitchen's warmth, your bungalow
grown quiet, the radio off and the earth waking up around us.

Photo courtesy of the League of Canadian Poets

Spirit of the City

KATHERINE L. GORDON

for Raymond Souster

From gutters to gargoyles
the teem of life swirls its stories,
the city stretches into every dimension
a poet dares to probe —
revealing the wonder of the ugly
the flickering strobe of beauty,
the interplay of dream and duty
that transfigures the observer
into the diamond and coal of all emotion.
A rare poet will harvest it all,
translate the restless stream into verses
to fill the heart of Everyman,
find a poem in a cardboard cringer
the be-decked of art and opera
blend the facets of human experience
into a glory of encompassing colour.
Such a man learns humility and grace
sees himself in every revelation.
Ray taught a generation to write of everything
in unrestricted form and line,
breathing the lyric of creation
with all its pain and ecstasy.
Love lay beneath insight, Ray exemplified it.
He asked no obituary, would never need one —
his spirit lives among us forever
in the growing entity of the gross and the gorgeous
the pitiful and pitiless
the love that surrounds each drama
that shapes his city.
Toronto, the meeting place of all the tribes
now his sacred site for poet pilgrims.

Parting Words from a Gentle Man

Norma West Linder

Being an avid fan throughout the 60s
of his careful observations of such moments
as elephants on Yonge Street, or a boy caught stealing —
a dream came true for me, I met Ray Souster

thanks to my love, a longtime friend of his
who took me to the Grenadier on Bloor Street
to shake hands with the man who first inspired me
to try my hand at poetry.

Though blind, I sensed that Ray could picture us,
feeling well pleased that he approved our union.
His mother's name was Norma, perhaps that helped
to make our meetings easy from the initial

visit to Toronto. More visits followed; we'd talk of jazz,
he'd play for us his latest acquisition.
Bill Evans was his favorite on piano
but he admired many great musicians.

When last we visited Ray's retirement home
I heard him say to James as we were leaving,
"Take care of Norma." I never dreamed that day
they'd be the final words we'd hear him speak.

The phrase "take care" is tossed off with abandon
but sometimes it can never be forgotten.

Parliament Street

Norma West Linder

the pink geranium
blooming in the window
between torn curtains
on the second floor left
doesn't do a thing
to help

Contact

Robert Currie

For Irving Layton and Raymond Souster

In the U. of S. bookstore, pricing texts for intersession,
I'm drawn to a wire rack, a rugged face, slashes of red
and gold across a thoughtful visage. I seize
the book, the price so low I know for sure
there's been a grave mistake, I rush
to the till, fling down my cash before
some harried clerk can raise the price.
On the first bench outside I begin
A Red Carpet for the Sun.

Wandering in the stacks where I once lost
all my powers of concentration, finding
Desmond Pacey's *Creative Writing in Canada*
bookmarked with what seemed to be a snapshot
of the German actress, Maria Schell, her smile
enough to melt ice from January windshields,
today I spot a pamphlet, yellowed pages
bound by staples, *When We Are Young*.

Tonight I jot down an image, play
with words, try to give them shape.
There's been no official diagnosis,
but already I know I'm afflicted
with a fever that I pray will
rage through all my days.

Ray Times

KENT BOWMAN

In memory of Ray Souster —
January 15, 1921 - October 19, 2012

High times! Jazz times!
Times comparing classic jazz encounters
and big band memories
when Toronto was a young jazz town.
Ray spoke of a tavern known as the "Town"
and that wretched night an infamous gambler
was beaten down in front of its respectable patrons,
ending a perfect venue for this fledgling art form.
Raymond Souster, a self-effacing holder
of a Governor General's Award and
possessor of the Order of Canada,
was just called Ray by his many friends.
In my mind, I still hear him answering his telephone
with "Hi me hardies," whenever I called him.
He was a man whose blindness never stopped
his prodigious outpouring of extraordinary poetry
reflecting a perceptive understanding of life's subtleties,
often unnoticed by others.

Travel

GEORGE FETHERLING

Ray Souster in memoriam

Back there our cheeks were
gouged by tears that rinsed our face of knowing.
Eyes weak from pleading, ears grown deaf to sirens,
earth overrun with data while here
the sky is full of context and clouds
provide perspective.

We had to go when things got skewed.
Gin was all we had for washing.
We cleaned our teeth with ashes
but the ashes being yours were sweet.

This is not departure but refusal to remain
not a leaving but an uncoming.

Best keep unread what was printed.
What the recto said to the verso is no one else's business.
Write it down and salt it well.
The proverbs lack the verbs they chaperone.

We're heading for that line beyond which
there is no more statute only case law
whenever events break one way and not another.

Ours is a haphazard journey to places
more random than I'm making them sound.

We'll travel till the country runs out of space
and all the witnesses have died.

This sensation of movement gives me
a dangerous confidence that stretches
noon all the way to midnight and unsolves old crimes.

History neatly tucked away, the splatter patterns
and the long trail of debris.

Stage fright? don't be silly. The audience
is afraid of *me*.

J'ai grandi en pleine cambrousse but no more
defiant acts of belonging.

I know a man who deals in second-hand names
and works both sides of the river.

The morgue is decorated for halloween.

Give me a number where I can reach you.

Ray drops by for tea

Karl Jirgens

There are two Rays,
the one I remember, and,
the one I drank tea with.

Ray drops by for a cup of tea.
Likes it piping hot. Black. No milk. No sugar.
He's been visiting kin across the street,
kitty corner from where I live, on Rivercrest Road.
My place is within walking distance of Ray's house,
over on Baby Point. He drops by sometimes.
Yonge Street banker. Dressed old-style.
Always unassuming. Enters wearing
patent leather black shoes, gleaming
with a whiff of R.C.A.F. shine.
We chat about imagism, and his latest book,
when my calico introduces herself,
rubbing past Ray's pant leg, as he takes a weight off,
atop the living room sofa.
We opine about Olson and Creeley, and
William Carlos Williams' many straw hats.
He parks his teacup on the coffee table,
"I have a cat *just* like that one."
I nod, pour more tea.
"Just like that one. Only mine's male,
and this one's female."
The cat arches low, clawing
into the aqua broadloom.
"Mind you, my cat's orange and white, and yours
is orange and *black* and white, but barring that,
they match each other to a T."
I stroke the calico along her spine,
offer a cookie.

"Although, mine's a short hair and,
yours is a long hair."
Rays of late afternoon sun arch low through the
front porch windows, warming our backs,
casting our shadows onto the broadloom.
"And this cat looks younger. Mine's older.
Other than that...
they're identical."
Ray reaches down, strokes the calico, while
I study the spine of his latest book.
"And my cat has brown eyes, while this one's
are green." The calico hops onto the couch where
Ray sits, sipping tea.
"They're exactly the same, though my cat has a bob-tail,
and one ear bent over. Otherwise,
you couldn't tell them apart."
The calico curls up for nap.
Ray smiles quietly,
cupping his mug.

Over a Shoulder

S.J. White

Surprised to find a poet among suits
and chosen by the place he lived;
his city blanket laid in picnic style
tryst of earth north of a great lake sea
naughty then but not the evil now —
a streetcar city in a cabbage town
finding shape from settlement and field
where he lingered in about its skirts.
Not footsteps but in fingerprints he wrote
as though the streets had been designed
to fit his peopled lines, his girly words
in conversations taken at their will
each a sudden turn…a burst of sunlight
caught of tedium's inconsequential days
and so we feel the aura that he knew
although we come from other dreams.

Grey Matter

BERNADETTE RULE

Even in colour photographs he looks black & white
as if photo-shopped in from an earlier era.
Behind the grey suit, the salt & pepper hair, the black-
rimmed glasses & paper-white skin, what Canadian
Bank of Commerce customer, livid with worry
about those beautiful blue, purple, green & pink bills —
not to mention the longed-for sepia —
what tortured twentieth century Torontonian
would ever have guessed at the prismatic poetry
locked deep in the vault of Raymond Souster's brain?

The Breakfast of Birds

Andreas Gripp

> "Each tree seems to have a bird in it singing
> Its fool head off"
> – Raymond Souster, *Night After Rain*

What sorrow is there
that can compare to joy
being found from the feasting
on worms,

the ecstasy of song
sprung from relentless rain
and the sighting of wriggling mud,

a budding willow to remind us
that happiness is indeed relative,
subject to taste and weather.

Souster's Haiku

ANDREAS GRIPP

Kiss of sleepy lips
Caterpillar on the wall
stroked by dawn of sun

Luminaries: Aubrey Street, North Bay

Laurie Kruk

> *The thin*
> *single light of a candle*
> *burning in the window.*
>
> *All the hope left*
> *in the world, one could say…*
>
> – Raymond Souster
> "The Light and the Flame" (*Hanging In*, 1979)

Passing by neighbourhood Christmas displays,
these lit-up, closed-up house-fronts
ringing in the season
with strings of bulbs, red velvet bows, gold-wire reindeer,
cardboard crèches, inflatable waving Santas
and giant spinning snowglobes, trailing
       extension cords —

then I stop, caught by
shocking spots of unelectric light
flames that flicker, flare
white on white on white

just candles, lit
in unmarked paper bags
planted in snowbanks
lining this side-street
on December 24th: whose
unclaimed gift?

flames that will burn all night
breath of golden heat
lit by unknown hands
venturing to the street

in the depth of four-thirty dusk
week after Winter Solstice:
whose hand, whose light
-ing? And whose will eventually reach out

to undo
each golden glow
settling within waxen wings
on slowly melting snow?

Someone or something that desires
to keep something fragile alive:
like our pet rabbit, coat matching the snow
who we feed, carry out and fence from harm
so we can window-watch him, and know
our piece
of this —

white winter fire
sheltered, striving, dancing
on a quiet road
at twenty below
near the longest night —

a testament to breath
its precious brevity
which will, I hope, outshine
all this world's de-light.

A Tip of the Hat to Raymond Souster

G.W. Down

Whether it was the way he traced the tint of
The plasterer's face, or tapped his Bay top hat
Tribute, or how he unveiled virtue
At the Dundas corner with Elizabeth,
He penned the city's streets, with precision scanned its beats
As though he holds
                eternal rights to the title
Toronto's Top-line Bard
                which by most squarely reasoned measures
He does.

Daylight My Darknesses
RYAN GIBBS

for Ray Souster

Riding a thundering horse
down Dundas and Elizabeth,
the banker sought inspiration
in the unspoken courage of
the girls at the corner.

He went back for Gwen
but never found her,
only stories that
she too was lost,
in some mad search
for stray alley cats.

What he discovered
was poetry
as elusive as
Queen Anne's Lace,
tiny prayers of comfort,
as he prepared for
a final journey
into darkness.

riding the horse/again

Terry Ann Carter

for better, or worse,
Raymond — I'm hooked —
hanging on any way I can
to those great white flanks
thundering down
your wide canyon
of sound

Ruby-Throated Hummingbird

ALLAN COOPER

It's okay for a poem to open in grief as long as something inside us wakens, shakes the dew from its wings, flies suddenly into the other world.

*

She waits, perched in the bare branches of the white roses. She has a light green feathered coat. Her eyes are small black beads. She sits a long time, turning her head quickly from side to side. When the time is right, she flies up, hovers near the feeder, lands, takes inside sips of cool nectar.

*

Imagine a nest small as a walnut that holds two magic beans. She sits there all day. The nest woven of lichens and webs opens like a flower as the young swell beneath her.

*

Her heart beats three-hundred times a minute. Imagine our hearts trembling like that. In the world of the ecstatic they say that it's true.

*

Late August. Now she is gone, to the left, to the right. She flies up and up in widening gyres, hovers one-hundred feet above the house, flies in a direct line south across the bay.

*

Yes, absence does make presence: small streaks of fire in the waiting air.

*

The dark thorns of my body will have to wait. Imagine the sweetness of the world in a single bead of dew. Imagine her hovering at the exact centre of the light.

Autumn Ducks, Five O'Clock

James Deahl

While the afternoon's chilly
and the wind's from the northwest
it's not quite November
nor is this Toronto,
still those ducks feeding
in the Humber River
so long ago are much like
the ones feeding today
on Lake Chipican — murky brown
waters, ice-cold on the edge of frost;
sky like solder, sun drifted
into the far, far west
over Michigan.

Soon the ducks will fly south
then return with spring's warmth
to mate — a type of
resurrection. Our lives
also leave and return
with a final resurrection
in Heaven.

Later tonight: a clear
cold sky, every star vivid
through my leaf-shorn walnut.
Such vast distances! There to here,
here to there, impossible
to ever comprehend
like those bobbing mallards
about to embark for Florida,
the West Indies.

Japanese Maple

James Deahl

a lament for Raymond Souster

One week before the Day of the Dead
the Japanese maple in my backyard
is almost too perfect, every leaf
incandescent enough to ignite the night
yet all remain unfallen. You, true master
of the backyard poem, will never see
this tree, nor my wisteria
blown yellow by the winds off Lake Huron.
Nor will we again discuss Robert Lowell
or Kenneth Patchen under your mulberry
during the dog days of a Toronto summer.

*May that day never come when we
finally say goodbye,* you wrote recently.
But that day did come and go a week ago.
In your last backyard poem you described
leaf-stripped trees facing the bitterness
of winter; today I see my black walnut
retains not one leaf as afternoon
welcomes late October's chill.

The First Poet . . . and the Foremost

JOHN ROBERT COLOMBO

for Donna Dunlop

He was the first poet I ever met. There were no poets in my hometown of Kitchener, where I was born and raised. But once I came to Toronto in the mid-1950s, I found it had a slew of bards and versifiers. I sought them out at the old Greenwich Gallery, where Raymond Souster held sway with the Contact Poetry series of regular public readings. In his own way he was a fine model and mentor, that way being his unqualified commitment to the art and craft of the muse of modernism as he saw it.

*

F.R. Scott, A.J.M. Smith, and A.M. Klein introduced literary modernism to Montreal and hence to Canada. In the company of Irving Layton and Louis Dudek, who formed the so-called Cerberus group, he established the beachhead for literary modernism on the Toronto shore of Lake Ontario. The exact site is the long-gone Sunnyside Amusement Park, its golden years celebrated in lively poem after lively poem.

*

I will never forget the shock that I experienced when I saw him behind bars, literally . . . the bars being those of the teller's cage in the vault in the murky basement of the old Canadian Bank of Commerce. Other Canadian poets have worked in banks, of course, including Robert W. Service and Earle Birney, not to mention T.S. Eliot, without deleterious effect. In common with them he would never be described as a banker or a securities officer by profession! When I appeared, he locked up the cage and we left the solemn building for sunlight and lunch at a diner near Queen and Yonge Streets. There is no doubt that the bank's securities were safe in Ray's hands even during his short, noon-hour absences.

*

During his lifetime he wanted no memorials: no plaques to mark his first house on Mayfield Avenue or his second on Baby Point Road; no sign to identify in any imaginative way the stairway in Willard Gardens in the district of Swansea where he used to enjoy the flowers and the fresh air. In a sense all of the city's West End was his fairground, for unlike any other writer he celebrated the vibrancy of its life and captured the colour of his times in his short, unassuming poems of surprising and unsurpassed lyricism.

*

Is there a bee that buzzes, a sparrow that chirps, a dandelion that bends in the wind, a street person who mutters, a lover who sighs in pleasure or in vain, a wife who is a helpmate, a politician or a businessman who is lacking in fellow feeling, a baseball pitcher who loses his pitching arm, a lieutenant who bonds with his fellow servicemen, an explorer for whom resolve is second-nature, a youngster who faces the future with fear, or an older poet who looks back on a lifetime of such memories? Yes there is and are.

*

Now his remains lie in an urn in the family's plot in Mount Pleasant Cemetery, in the central part of the city, somewhat far from the city's West End which he had made so much his own. Yet in this way he has staked his claim to the entirety of the City of Toronto, now and for times to come.

*

Yes, he was the first poet I ever met, and he remains the foremost.

December 3, 2012

Raymond Souster and contributor Michael Fraser.

Photo by Dori Mould

Contributors

Steven Michael Berzensky (Mick Burrs) is a poetry enthusiast and editor. He oversaw the literary magazine *Grain* (1988-1990) and founded the Annual Short Grain Contest. He co-edited with Allan Briesmaster the anthology *Crossing Lines: Poets Who Came to Canada in the Vietnam War Era* (Seraphim, 2008). He has won many literary awards for his poetry, including the 1998 Saskatchewan Book Award for Poetry for *Variations on the Birth of Jacob* (Muses Co., 1997). Recent videos featuring Mick will be found on YouTube, including "Real Live Poet" and "Reunion with Terry Gilliam."

Kent Bowman was encouraged to write poetry by Ted Plantos. In 2007, his essay on "The Creative Process (Songwriting, Composing, Writing Poetry)" was accepted by *Imagination in Action*. In 2008, he contributed "Plate Spinning in America" to *Crossing Lines: Poets Who Came to Canada in the Vietnam War Era*. In 2009, *And Left a Place to Stand On* accepted "Zen River Memories." In 2010, his collection, *On the Other Side of Paradise*, was published.

Ronnie R. Brown is an Ottawa writer. She has had work published in over 100 magazines/anthologies. The author of six books of poetry, Brown was the 2006 winner of The Acorn-Plantos People's Poetry Award for *States of Matter* (Black Moss Press, 2005). Her most recent collection is *Rocking on the Edge* (Black Moss, 2010).

Terry Ann Carter is the author of five collections of poetry and four haiku chapbooks. *Lighting the Global Lantern: A Teacher's Guide to Writing Haiku and Related Literary Forms* (Wintergreen Studios Press, 2011) is used in Canadian classrooms. She is the president of Haiku Canada.

John Robert Colombo assisted Ray with the original Contact Poetry Reading Series at the old Greenwich Gallery. *All the Poems of John Robert Colombo* appeared in three volumes in 2006.

Allan Cooper's fourteenth book of poems, *The Deer Yard*, was co-written with Nova Scotia poet Harry Thurston. He has won the Bailey Prize twice, the Peter Gzowski Award, and was short listed for the CBC Literary Awards three times. He has recently completed a translation of Rainer Maria Rilke's *Duino Elegies*. He spends much of the year in Alma, New Brunswick, a small fishing village on the Bay of Fundy.

Robert Currie, who lives in Moose Jaw, served two terms as Saskatchewan's third Poet Laureate. He was honoured in 2009 when he received the Saskatchewan Lieutenant Governor's Award for Lifetime Achievement in the Arts. His most recent books are *Witness* (poetry, Hagios Press, 2009) and *Living with the Hawk* (novel, Thistledown Press, 2013).

James Deahl is a friend of Raymond Souster.

David Donnell was born in St. Marys, Ontario and lives in Toronto. He won the Governor General's Award for Poetry for *Settlements* in 1983.

G.W. Down is a poet, lyricist, editor and business consultant who lives in Hamilton, Ontario. He is also a partner in The Book Band, a company which does marketing, distribution and promotion for Canadian publishers.

Margaret Patricia Eaton's poem "Battle of Britain" was selected from her first collection, *Seeking Grace* (2006), which recounts her mother's experiences as a W.W. II nurse. She's also the author of *Painted Poems* (2008) and *Vision & Voice* (2011) which contains "Celtic Trilogy," first place winner in the WFNB 2009 poetry competition. A free-lance writer and photographer from Moncton, NB, she feels most honoured to be included in this tribute anthology.

David Eso is a poet and graduate student at the University of Calgary, studying the letters of Robert Kroetsch with Dr. Aritha van Herk. Eso's poems, articles, interviews and reviews unite Canada's literary heritage with its impending renaissance.

Chris Faiers' recent books are *Eel Pie Island Dharma* and *Zen River: Poems & Haibun*. VN War resister, gravedigger, hippie, steelworker, jailbird, union rep, commie, cook, founder of Unfinished Monument Press, haijin, meditator, real estate, village librarian, Main St. Library Poetry, Purdy Country Literary Festivals, steward Zen River Gardens, shaman, 100+ mags and anthos, 19 collections, 64 & still truckin' ...

George Fetherling is a poet, novelist and cultural commentator who lives in Toronto and Vancouver. Recent books include *The Sylvia Hotel Poems* and *Walt Whitman's Secret*.

Joe Fiorito is an author and a city columnist at the *Toronto Star* newspaper.

Michael Fraser is a high school teacher, poet, and writer. He has been published in various anthologies and journals including: *Literary Review of Canada*, *The Paris Atlantic*, and *Caribbean Writer*. His manuscript, *The Serenity of Stone*, won the 2007 Canadian Aid Literary Award Contest and was published in 2008 by Bookland Press. He won *Arc*'s 2012 Readers' Choice Poem of the Year. He is the creator and director of the Plasticine Poetry Series.

Ryan Gibbs is an English professor in Sarnia, Ontario, whose poems have appeared in *Illumen*, *Beyond Centauri*, *The Country Connection Magazine*, and *Tower Poetry*, as well as anthologies *The Saving Bannister* (Canadian Authors Association) and *Whisky Sour City* (Black Moss Press).

Katherine L. Gordon is a rural Ontario poet enjoying an international connection to contemporary poetry through her books, anthologies, and reviews.

Andreas Gripp is the author of 17 books of poetry, including *Selected Poems 2000-2012* (Harmonia Press, 2013). He lives in London, Ontario. His work has been published in a number of literary magazines and anthologies, including *Ascent Aspirations, Tower Poetry, Literary Review of Canada, Carousel, Descant, Van Gogh's Ear,* and *Quern: An Anthology of Contemporary Poets.*

Debbie Okun Hill is President of The Ontario Poetry Society and a recent Ontario Arts Council Writers' Reserve grant recipient. Her poems have been published in *Descant, Existere, Vallum,* and *The Windsor Review* in Canada plus *Möbius, The Binnacle,* and *Still Point Arts Quarterly* in the US. Black Moss Press will publish her first full collection in the Fall 2013.

Laurence Hutchman has just retired from the Université de Moncton in Edmundston, where he taught language and literature for twenty-three years. He has published eight collections of poetry including *Foreign National, Emery, Beyond Borders, Selected Poems,* and *Reading the Water.* His most recent book is *In the Writers' Words: Conversations with Eight Canadian Poets.* In 2007 he received the Alden Nowlan Award for Excellence in English-language Literary Arts.

Karl Jirgens is the former Head of the English Department at the University of Windsor, where he currently serves as associate professor. Jirgens is the author of four books, including, *Strappado* (Coach House), *A Measure of Time* (Mercury), *Bill Bissett and His Works,* and *Christopher Dewdney and His Works* (ECW). He has edited *Rampike*, an international literary journal, since 1979.

Laurie Kruk was born in Toronto. She currently teaches English at Nipissing University in North Bay. Her poetry has been published in over twenty literary and academic journals or anthologies, culminating in three collections: *Theories of the World* (Netherlandic, 1992), *Loving the Alien* (YSP, 2006) and *My Mother Did Not Tell Stories* (Demeter, 2012).

Dennis Lee lives in Toronto, where he is a resident artist at Soulpepper Theatre.

Norma West Linder is the author of 5 novels, 14 collections of poetry, a memoir of Manitoulin Island, a children's book, a biography of Pauline McGibbon, and well over 100 short stories, many published internationally and aired over CBC Radio. For 24 years she taught English at Lambton College. Linder wrote a weekly column for *The Observer* for seven years. Her selected poems, *Adder's-tongues*, was edited by James Deahl. A collection of her short fiction, *No Common Thread*, was published 2013.

Bruce Meyer is author of 34 books and is the Poet Laureate for the City of Barrie. He is Professor of English at Georgian College and also teaches at Victoria College in the University of Toronto.

Brian Purdy was born on September 28, 1948, Belleville, Ontario, the son of A.W. Purdy. He left the Univ. of Toronto for casual labor while self-educating. He wrote lyrics for lp *The Lion and the Lady* during early 1970s and published *To Feed the Sun, Interloper, Strips,* and *Poet's Garden* with many appearances in magazines and several in anthologies. He also draws and paints.

Bernadette Rule's most recent poetry collection is *The Literate Thief: Selected Poems* (Larkspur Press, Monterey, Ky. 2007). She also edited the book *Remember Me to Everybody: Letters From India, 1944 to 1949* by Frederick Gower Turnbull (West Meadow Press, 1997) and *In the Wings: Stories of Forgotten Women* (Seraphim Editions, 2012). Her manuscript entitled *Gardening At the Mouth of Hell* (West Meadow, 1996) won the 1991 Poetry Prize at the Eden Mills Writers' Festival. Rule hosts the weekly arts-interview program, Art Waves (archive.org/details/artwaves).

Simcha (Sam) Simchovitch was born in the Jewish *shtetl* of Otwock, Poland. Sam is the only member of his large family to survive the Holocaust. He writes and publishes in both Yiddish and English, and has been awarded major literary prizes for his books in both languages. Sam's many poetry collections include *A Song Will Remain: Selected Poems* and the two-volume *The Fiery Mountain: Collected Poems*.

Glen Sorestad is the author of well over 20 books and chapbooks of poetry, has appeared in over 60 anthologies and texts and his poems have been translated into seven languages. A Life Member of both the League of Canadian Poets and the Saskatchewan Writers Guild and a Member of the Order of Canada, Sorestad and his wife Sonia live in Saskatoon.

Lynn Tait is an award-winning poet/photographer residing in Sarnia, Ont. Her poems have appeared in numerous American and Canadian magazines including *Windsor Review, Quills, Contemporary Verse 2, Feathertale Review,* and in over 60 anthologies. She is a member of the League of Canadian Poets, The Ontario Poetry Society, and 2 local writing groups: Writers in Transition and After Hours Poets.

S.J. White has written non-fiction most of his life and short stories and poetry over the last thirty years. He has published four books plus numerous chapbooks and is published in the usual literary journals and anthologies. He is retired and lives with his wife in Brantford.

Carleton Wilson is a poet, editor, publisher, and book designer. His first book, *The Material Sublime*, was published by Nightwood Editions in 2011. He lives and works in the Junction, Toronto.

Michael Wurster is the author of three poetry collections: *The Cruelty of the Desert*, *The Snake Charmer's Daughter*, and *The British Detective*. Wurster won *Pittsburgh Magazine*'s inaugural Harry Schwalb Excellence in the Arts Award. He lives in Pittsburgh where he teaches at the Pittsburgh Center for the Arts School.

Anna Yin won the 2005 Ted Plantos Memorial Award and the 2010 MARTY Award. She has three older chapbooks and *Wings Toward Sunlight* in print. Her new book *Inhaling the Silence* was published in 2013. She was a finalist for Canada's Top 25 Canadian Immigrants Award in 2011/2012. Her poems have been broadcast on CBC Radio, Rogers TV and Chinese TV stations. More at annapoetry.com.

Raymond Souster and editor James Deahl at the Grenadier Retirement Residence. This is probably the final photo taken of Ray. He was 91.

Photo by Norma West Linder

Acknowledgements

Ronnie R. Brown's poem "For Keeps" was originally published in 2005 by Black Moss Press in her book *States of Matter*.

Robert Currie's poem "Contact" was originally published in 2006 by Coteau Books in his book *Running in Darkness*.

Margaret Patricia Eaton's poem "Battle of Britain — 1940" was originally published in 2006 by Eagles' Wings Press in her book *Seeking Grace*.

Andreas Gripp's poem "The Breakfast of Birds" was originally published in 2013 by Harmonia Press in his book *The Breakfast of Birds*.

Dennis Lee's three poems were originally published in 1993 by Brick Books in his book *Riffs*.

Norma West Linder's poem "Parliament Street" was originally published in 2012 by Aeolus House in her book *Adder's-tongues: A Choice of Norma West Linder's Poems*.

Simcha Simchovitch's poems "Raymond Souster" and "Downtown" were originally published in 1996 by Lugus Publications in his book *A Song Will Remain: Selected Poems*. "Raymond Souster" later appeared in *The Fiery Mountain: Collected Poems*.

Carleton Wilson's poem "Unlimited Variations on the Avro Lancaster" was originally published in 2011 by Nightwood Editions (nightwoodeditions.com) in his book *The Material Sublime*.

Michael Wurster's poem "Stella By Starlight" was originally published in 2000 by Elemenope Productions in his book *The Snake Charmer's Daughter*. His "Newsboy" was originally published in 2009 by Main Street Rag Publishing in his book *The British Detective*.

All poems are reprinted by permission of their authors and/or their publishers. The editor wishes to thank the original publishers for permission to use these poems in this tribute anthology.

The editor also wishes to recognize the sound advice he received during the writing of his Introduction from Souster scholars Hugh Cook, Bruce Whiteman, and Terry Barker. They were helpful in improving the accuracy and style of the version printed here.

Ray beside the Humber River

Toronto Star Archive Photo taken by Sharon Godfrey Oct. 4, 1984
Credit: Toronto Star

Other Quattro Poetry Books

And the cat says… by Susan L. Helwig
Against the Flight of Spring by Allan Briesmaster
The Rules of the Game by Ludwig Zeller
Too Much Love by Gianna Patriarca
parterre by elías carlo
Night-Eater by Patricia Young
Fermata by Dennison Smith
Little Empires by Robert Colman
nunami by Barbara Landry
One False Move by Tim Conley
Where the Terror Lies by Chantel Lavoie
Something Small To Carry Home by Isa Milman
jumping in the asylum by Patrick Friesen
Without Blue by Chris D'Iorio
When the Earth by Lisa Young
And tell tulip the summer by Allan Graubard
Book of Disorders by Luciano Iacobelli
Saugeen by Rob Rolfe
Strong Bread by Giovanna Riccio
Rough Wilderness by Rosemary Aubert
hold the note by Domenico Capilongo
syrinx and systole by Matthew Remski
Sew Him Up by Beatriz Hausner
Psychic Geographies and Other Topics by Gregory Betts
The Sylvia Hotel Poems by George Fetherling
Ten Thousand Miles Between Us by Rocco de Giacomo
A River at Night by Paul Zemokhol
This Is How I Love You by Barbara Landry
Looking at Renaissance Paintings by Caroline Morgan Di Giovanni
The Hawk by Rob Rolfe
My Etruscan Face by Gianna Patriarca
Garden Variety edited by Lily Contento
MIC CHECK edited by David Silverberg
Evidence by Samuel Andreyev
Interstellar by Allan Briesmaster